This book is dedicated to my
children, Jesse and Rainee Lyleson, and to all the children of the world.
May they inherit a world rich in unspoiled natural beauty.

First Published by Avalon Books 1993

16/8-12 Pacific Parade, Dee Why, NSW 2099, Australia
Telephone (02) 971 4441

Produced by Rob Bayley Design
Surry Hills, NSW, Australia

Typeset by Asset Typesetting Pty Ltd,
Leichhardt, NSW, Australia

Printed in Singapore by Kyodo Printing Co. Ltd.



ISBN 0 696 13442 6

# Reflections from Down Under

Text and Photography
by
Eric Lyleson

AVALON BOOKS

## *ACKNOWLEDGEMENTS*

*I would like to give thanks to my loving partner Lisa Peers whose support and critical feedback fuelled my persistence and kept me true to my vision of this book. Many thanks to my writing coach, editing assistant and dear friend Bob Klein who has helped me find my style and bring what I have to say into sharper focus. Thanks to Malcolm Cohan and Susan Hayward whose example and encouragement let me know it was possible. Thanks to the countless people who have told me it's worthwhile putting it into print. Thanks to Rob Bayley who brought it all together. Much appreciation to Richard Hoff and Yana Slade who introduced me to the path of self discovery in the wilderness. Deepest gratitude to Mom and Dad who have backed me all along in every way they could.*

*I'd like to thank some of the many authors who have inspired and guided me over the years with their writings: Carlos Castaneda, Lynn Andrews, Steven Foster and Meredith Little, Joseph Golstein and Jack Kornfield, Shakti Gawain, Milton Erickson, Steven Levine, Osho (Bagwan Shree Rajneesh), and especially to the companion on my travels; A Course in Miracles.*

*following my appreciation of the beauty of nature,*
*I'm led to the recognition of the nature of my beauty.*

MY EXPERIENCES in nature have always been a private, intimate affair, not often shared or spoken about. Intimacy is best achieved one to one. Although spending time with friends in nature is uplifting, it is in solitude that I have realised a deeper, more intimate connection with nature and myself.

During my many years of learning to appreciate nature and be nurtured by her beauty, I never wanted a camera; I practiced being *with* her, rather than *doing* something to her. To be intimate with nature, I thought, I must always devote my full attention, and not engage in extraneous activities.

Then a couple of close friends shared their wilderness photography with me. I was moved by the magic they captured on film. Their love of nature shone from the photos, reminding me of my love, and inspired me to spend more time outdoors. Before I set off for Australia, I purchased a camera and delved into the art of photography.

Having a camera altered my approach to the wilderness. I became a hunter of beauty, tracking down artistic or poetic photographs. In looking for photos, I began seeing my surroundings in new ways. This attitude sharpened my senses and expanded my awareness. I was more alert to what might lay hidden in a stream, in a cliff face or behind a dense curtain of foliage. I would wait hours for the light to change, or go out of my way for interesting perspectives, hoping to capture some hidden beauty at a special moment. There were places I would never have explored if I hadn't been looking for a photograph.

Seeking different perspectives is one of the keys to personal growth. Without fresh viewpoints we tend to project past experiences into our present perceptions. With limited and coloured information, we perceive few choices and habitually live our lives in the same old ways. The more viewpoints we have about anything, the more we see of it, giving us more information, which in turn increases our understanding, leaving us with more informed choices about how to live our lives.

My camera was training me to seek different viewpoints for all of my life. But taking photos became addictive at times. It was important to remind myself to put the camera down and just be with nature. Wherever my camera led me, I worked on maintaining a balance between *observing* the beauty of my environment, and opening my heart and intimately *experiencing* it.

We are approaching the brink of worldwide environmental disaster. The vibrant pristine planet our ancestors inhabited has continually been plundered, tamed, abused and taken for granted as part of our strategy for survival and security. However, if we are to survive as a species, we need to cultivate more intimate and harmonious relationships with all of our planetary cohabitants — oceans, rivers, mountains, deserts, valleys, animals, trees, rocks, plants and people. It is much harder to hurt the ones we know, understand and love intimately, than the ones we consider strangers and remain distant from and frightened of.

It is my hope that these photographs, stories and poems offer a different view of the world we live in. May you be inspired to explore wild places wherever you live or travel; put aside your expectations and usual ways of approaching nature and open yourself to a deeper, more intimate and loving relationship with Mother Earth.

I ARRIVED at Wilson's Promontory in the late afternoon with just enough daylight to hike down the coastline trail to Oberon Bay. After a couple of weeks in Melbourne, I was anxious to return to the wilderness again. As I hurried down the trail, most of my surroundings and what were probably inspiring ocean views went unnoticed. Instead my mind raced ahead with thoughts of finding a campsite, making dinner, destinations beyond Wilson's Prom., and so on.

"Wait a minute," I said, stopping mid-stride, "Is this hcw I want to spend my time?"

I closed my eyes, took a few deep breaths and let my awareness go inward. A fertile moment of silence gave birth to a declaration of my intentions, "I want to explore nature's beauty and expand my appreciation of it. I want to gain a deeper understanding of who I am through solitary communication with nature. I want to let go of the fears, anxieties and preconceptions that hold me back from experiencing the true magnificence of life."

I stepped back into the inner silence before opening my eyes. The world already looked different. I became aware of the subtle green hues of the leaves on the various forms of coastal foliage, the patterns of light and dark created by the interplay of filtered light and shadow cast by the sun as it neared the horizon. In the furry bark of a weather-battered tree, I could see the oultine of an old Aboriginal man's face surrounded by grey swirls of his unkempt beard and hair.

Making my way down the trail, mundane thoughts still floated through my mind, but they no longer blinded me to the evening's splendour. Now that I had stopped worrying, I remembered that it was a full moon night. There would be plenty of light to make camp, no matter how late I stopped. In the last light of dusk, I set up camp in a protected forest glen behind the sand dunes of Oberon Bay.

On the beach, a mild sea-breeze caressed my ears with a soft hum. The leaves of low growing trees shimmered with reflected moonlight, like the rippled surface of a mountain lake. I fixed my gaze on the moon and anchored my bare feet in the cool sand. The longer I concentrated on the moon, the more my thoughts and surroundings blurred into insignificance. Moonlight flooded my inner being.

After some time, my legs began vibrating. I tried walking to move the energy, but when I turned away from the moon, I felt uncomfortable. I stopped and returned my gaze upward and began rotating my weight back and forth in a Tai Chi-like dance. A pressure swelled in my chest as my movements expanded. I vaulted into a passionate modern ballet of prancing, leaping and pirouetting along the calm water's edge. But annoying inner voices infiltrated my rapture, "That's enough now!," they said, "What if someone sees you? Are you mad? Who do you think you are?"

The voices felt like shackles, tightening around my arms and legs. "Let me go!", I shouted. But with laboured breath I fell to the sand, defeated. It was a familiar feeling and recurring pattern for me. So often, when I have followed my heart, giving myself permission to do what I most wanted, those fearful and restricting inner voices have sabotaged my possible successes.

I sobbed with grief, as memories of missed opportunities and failures in sports, relationships, schooling and career surfaced. Curled up on the sand I gently rocked myself for comfort. As time passed, the movement expanded to rolling around on my back, on to my belly, back to my back and then over my shoulder on to my feet. The movement gradually softened into a timid dance. Tears of joy flowed from my heart as I experienced a new sense of freedom. The dance eventually wound down to a slow silent walk into the face of the moon, and then back to camp. Over the next few days in the park, and during my travels through different wilderness areas, I continued the ritual of stating my intentions. This empowered my journey with greater meaning and opened the door to new possibilities, rather than continuing to approach the wilderness and life in habitually unconscious ways. When I got lost in old patterns of feeling separate from the beauty and wonder of life, I took notice of these experiences and because of my stated intentions, I accepted them as opportunities to learn new ways of relating to myself and the world.

AS I HITCHHIKED towards Mount Kosciusko, the roads were empty. As it is a large national park and home of the tallest mountain in Australia, I expected hordes of holiday makers loaded down with fishing, camping and camera gear. But summer is the off season here. It's the winter that lures thousands to the country's major ski resorts.

It was early afternoon when I walked into Guthega Ski Resort from Smiggin Holes. From here I followed a trail around a small reservoir and continued up above the south bank of the Snowy River. The trail, scratched in the dry grass between low growing shrubs, wound its way over the hills. I crossed the streams that rendezvoused with the river below. A flock of high flying birds settled in a cluster of Snow Gums on the ridge above me. The afternoon shadows were getting longer when I pitched camp by a cross-country ski hut.

I'd heard there were good-sized trout in the river so I dropped my line in, but I had little patience and even less success. The evening shadows grew into darkness. I huddled around my campfire as the temperature dropped significantly. My firewood pile dwindled rapidly, forcing me into my frigid tent and lightweight sleeping bag.

Bundled up in every piece of clothing I had, feeling cold and lonely, I voiced, "Why am I doing this?" No immediate answer came to mind.

I managed to stay just warm enough to maintain a fragile sleep. At the first hint of dawn I emerged from my tent (which was frozen solid) into an awakening landscape covered by a blanket of frost. I stayed warm with a cup of tea by the fire until the sun appeared through the snow gums of the ridgetop. As its warming rays melted the frosted meadow into millions of sparkling jewels, my thawing heart had the answer to my question.

I set off downhill and crossed the river on a swinging bridge. The trail soon disappeared into scrubby brush. I cut a path in the general direction of Mount Kosciusko, which was not visible to me. The climb was steep, my pack heavy, and the ground soggy from snow-melt. I stopped often to catch my breath, admiring the expansive views and the late summer wildfowers adorning the hillsides.

I had lunch at Blue Lake, a small, very blue glacial lake that's home to a unique species of freshwater shrimp. After exploring the shoreline, I followed the ridge trail up past a couple of waterfalls and small alpine lakes. At 6000 feet, I was well above the tree-line, giving me an unobstructed view of these ancient mountains, worn down over countless centuries.

I reached the main dividing ridge and for the first time was able to look out over the mountains and valleys that stretched out in a blue mist towards the western horizon.

A cold wind pushed a thickening grey mist around me, transforming a sunny summer day into winter. I hurried up the peak before struggling down a steep, overgrown trail marked sporadically by camouflaged posts which soon disappeared in the dimming light.

I felt relieved to reach the tree-line and my first stand of stunted snow gums. I collected just enough firewood to cook my dinner as the last grey light drained from the cloudy sky.

The following day was a steep descent following connecting spurs in and out of the forest shadows. I spotted brightly coloured Rosellas, but there were many other birds that I only heard from behind the dense foliage. After a rest, I discovered a long tail feather of a Lyrebird. The Lyrebird is a large, shy, ground bird that confuses its predators by emitting an assortment of bird-call imitations. The feather still serves to remind me, when I'm lost in cold despair, of the sparkles of joyfulness yet to come.

*Standing on darkness,*
*ice-fields of dread,*
*There they*
*slumbered, till light*
*raised his head.*

*The dawning of*
*illumination*
*Shines away frozen*
*resignation.*

*As it brings sparkles*
*of joyfulness,*
*To melt fear's icy*
*dew into bliss.*

THE CONSTANT erosion from surf, wind and rain has sculpted the limestone coast of Port Campbell into towering cliffs, natural arches and the island monoliths known as "The Twelve Apostles".

Besides the awesome beauty, a comforting and soft essence rests in the landscape. I wondered about the namesake "The Twelve Apostles". "Were these limestone giants standing together in a silent declaration of peace?" My friend Graham and I were navigated by a gentle, relaxed calm through the coastal shrubs atop the high rise bluffs. We stopped often to breathe in the views that stretched out towards Antarctica and to soak up the sun's soothing warmth.

As I walked, my hands brushed lightly over the various low-growing bushes. One variety, a type of salt bush, was particularly comforting to my touch. On an impulse, I stripped off my day pack and let myself fall backwards into this billowy pale grey cloud of a bush. My fall was cushioned by what felt like a soft, yet very supportive, mound of fluffy cotton. As I relaxed into the bush, it conformed to the contours of my body, supporting my weight perfectly. I felt as though I was resting in the hands of God, filled me with a deep sense of peace and belonging.

Graham and I spent the rest of the afternoon apart, strolling along the coastline while sampling the different 'comfort' bushes along the way. Later we remarked how each bush was different and yet so comfortable.

That night we camped on the shore of a small tidal inlet just east of the park. The next morning was gloomy and overcast, with blustery winds and only a sprinkle of moisture in the air. I trudged against the salty wind, up and down the tall sand dunes, while picking my way around and through bushes that scratched at my skin and clothing.

When I reached the exposed coastline, I was amazed at the sharp contrast between the peaceful quality of Port Campbell, which was visible up the coast, and these cliffs, which seemed to have been beaten and tortured into menacing shapes and gargoyle-like faces. The sparse foliage that survived on these ledges looked as if it had been scarred from doing battle with a fierce enemy. In retaliation, the plants had armed themselves with sharp swords and spiny barbs to defend their fragile hold on life.

With my arms spread wide like wings, I leaned into the wind that buffeted my face and body. I was nearly lifted into flight from my precipitous perch as I embraced its force. I roared with abandon, as a surge of power burst from my lungs. Like many other intense experiences, when I open myself to the wind I am invigorated and when I resist it, I end up feeling drained.

I sought shelter in a small cave set in the cliff face below. Despite facing directly into the wind it was remarkably calm. I sat and meditated on the distant horizon that was framed by the grimacing mouth of the cave. In my silence I realized how vital the balance of comfort and challenge were in my life. In comfort, I learn to relax and trust myself and my place in the universe; the challenge of hardship keeps me moving beyond my preconceptions and the complacency of old limitations, onto new experiences and greater understanding.

As the sky and ocean meet on the horizon, comfort and challenge seem to meet at the thin line I walk when I'm living life to the fullest.

WHILE OUT to dinner in Milton, on the south coast of New South Wales, I asked my new friends how to reach the Budawang Mountains. I was introduced to Bill and Tina who lived at the base of the mountains, and they invited me to their home for the night.

In the morning, I followed the Clyde River downstream to where it crossed the trail into the park. I ascended the trail through the forest to the base of the escarpment, then climbed up to a fortress-like rock formation known as The Castle. From this lookout I gazed across the valley at another prominent point known as Pigeon House. The Castle had been an Aboriginal men's ceremonial site and Pigeon House, which, from a distance, resembles a woman's breast, was the women's site. But it was The Castle and what lay beyond that had beckoned me.

Atop The Castle, I danced in sacred silence, feeling the power of its strategic position in the soles of my feet. A whisper of wind suggested I move along, and I followed a hint of a trail up a narrow ravine. The bluish rock bathed me in its cool aura as I squeezed through a secret passageway into what felt like a lost world. I picked my way through a maze of undefined tracks and soon found myself in the midst of convoluted rock faces and cone-like monoliths. The deeper I moved into the silence of this uncivilized land, the more I sensed the whispers of forgotten mysteries that lay embedded in the weathered rock.

To protect this delicate environment, no camping is allowed in the valley. So I followed a small creek over a narrow pass. Walking in the shadow of the sheer rock wall, I came to a couple of concave hollows that may have served as campsites for thousands of years. I collected firewood and water, and settled in for the night.

Sitting on a rock, in the crack between day and night, my eyes swallowed the last drop of sunlight before it evaporated into night. It wasn't long before the valley filled with silver light from the rising moon. The solar warmth emanating from the stone backdrop kept me comfortable in the cool night. I felt that these stone walls, if they could speak, would echo the stories told by the pilgrims that rested here. In that moment, I had a vision of myself as a member of a small Aboriginal hunting party in search of fresh game. In the shelter of the cliffs we sang and danced, spinning tales of previous trips and local spirits. I fell asleep in the protective custody of my translucent companions who rested under the blanket of darkness that covered the rock.

In the morning I scaled a dry waterfall which led me back to Monolith Valley. Exploring the sculpted domes, I descended into a steep crevice, where a hidden passageway took me into a dark mossy grotto. Filtered green light dimly lit a spring-fed pool which reflected my inward calm with clarity, as I sat in meditative silence.

It was nearly noon when I slid down the backside of this mountain plateau. I followed Angel Creek until I reached the brink of Crooked Falls, which plummets 100 metres to the valley below.

At dusk, after a steep descent, I made camp at the junction of two merging streams. In the twilight, I followed a gut feeling to a spot midstream, sat down between two rocks, and instantly felt at home. In restful anticipation, I greeted the amber moon, as it gradually entered the glowing, star-filled V, outlined by the tall gum trees flanking the creek. Listening to the gurgling serenade of the rising moon, I thought about building a fire and cooking dinner. But another voice said, "No. Just sit here a while longer."

This inner dialogue repeated itself throughout the evening. Each time my mind suggested I do something — build a fire, eat, read — my body declined. As the night flowed on, I thought about my

city life, always rushing, keeping busy, trying to be a part of what's happening, not wanting to feel left out, always seeking fulfilment outside myself. Here I was feeling totally happy, at one with the world, doing absolutely nothing, all alone in the illuminated peacefulness of the night. I realized there is nothing I need to do to be happy. It is actually the very activities I think will bring me happiness that, instead, distract me from my inner peace.

Joy and inner peace are our natural inheritance. It is our own beliefs, expectations and perceptions that send us blindly searching down dead end trails, trying to find out what is already waiting in the quiet moonlit night of our inner selves.

When I finally laid down that night and closed my eyes, moonlight filled my vision, and my heart glowed in peaceful celebration.

*Lightly I tread with conviction,*
*On polished stone*
*glazed by the greenness of life.*

*The bestower*
*of all existence*
*Presses at my footholds*
*of understanding,*

*Urging me*
*to more intimacy*
*With the vastness*
*of life everlasting.*

*here in the wilderness*
*the circle of life, death and rebirth surrounds me.*

JUST OUTSIDE Canberra, in the foothills of the Snowy Mountains, the sheer rock outcroppings of Bundanoon are known internationally by rock climbers. Hitchhiking out of Canberra, I was picked up by a couple of German climbers, Michael and Peter. They took me climbing on the granite cliffs which, most of the time, required finger tip grips.

We camped together that night, but in the morning they went back to the rocks while I followed a kangaroo trail into the forest. I kept to the ridges of the rolling wooded hills that were marked periodically with monuments of large rounded boulders. These boulders served as rest stops and vista points from which to survey the outlying hillsides and valleys. Down in a ravine I spotted several kangaroos, but they quickly bounded out of camera range.

Up to this point, walking through the eucalyptus forest had been fairly easy. But at the lower elevation, I encountered dense thickets of thorny bushes that scratched my arms and snagged my pack and clothing. The kangaroos must have had a good chuckle over this slow, top-heavy creature who trudged through the terrain they so gracefully traversed.

Several hours later I emerged from the forest canopy, revealing an afternoon sky subdued by a thin grey cloud cover. I continued my downhill trek through a series of forest meadows. I reached the bank of a small river as darkness descended and, with some difficulty, located a level campsite in the rocky terrain.

A soft blanket of clouds
Comforts the night
In darkness and cool warmth.

Simple amber flames,
Glow alone in the heart
Of dancing shadows.

Whispering winds above
Improvise with the steady chant
Of water over rocks below.

Providing the rhythm section
For the melody of nightbirds, crickets,
And other soloists of the night.

I awoke clouded with melancholy after having dreamt about my ex-wife. I was still grieving the loss of our marriage. Most of the day was spent in quiet reflection as I explored the humble beauty of this narrow river valley. That evening my melancholy matured into the familiar heartache I had known intimately since our relationship had begun to sour years before. I sang songs that usually helped me release my sadness, but on this night they only deepened the feeling and my tears flowed freely.

Nervous agitation cut my grieving short as I began pacing restlessly around the campfire. My pacing evolved into cathartic chanting and dancing. Winded and sweaty, I began pounding a log drum as my angry chants turned into pleas for mercy. Finally, my blistered hands dropped the sticks into the weakening flames and my heart cried out in anguish to be healed.

I stayed up late, gazing hypnotically into the glowing ashes of disintegrating logs. Eventually I fell into a restless sleep filled with dreams of fear and failure. The last two dream sequences before awakening, were my ex-wife telling me, "Guys like you will always be chasing after women like me," followed by my trying fruitlessly to dam up a set of rapids in a stream with rocks from the shore.

While meditating, a line from a Bee Gee's song (*If I can't have you, I don't want nobody baby*) played continuously through my head. I realized this was a reflection of the internal belief that perpetuated my attachment to my ex-wife, thereby maintaining my heartache and keeping me from opening up to love. I had been feeling empty and incomplete without her for over a year, and I now wanted to take a positive step towards regaining my wholeness and power.

There is a Native American practice of constructing a medicine doll as a way of re-owning one's personal power. I decided to make a symbolic image of this woman to whom I was giving so much of my reason for living. It would represent the qualities I felt was lacking in myself and my life.

Down by the river, I cut a small willow branch for the doll's torso and limbs, symbolizing her strong and flexible dancer's body. The legs I sharpened to pointed feet, like a ballerina. I stripped off all the leaves except for a few young buds that became her hands, symbolic of her artistic and creative abilities. Between two rocks grew a lovely delicate purple wildflower, the right size and shape for her head. Purple had been her favourite colour and I was often dazzled by her delicate beauty. Nearby stood a hardy wild rose bush laden with ripe rosehips. I attached two of these with a length of sinewy grass for her lovely full breasts, which I had always seen as a source of comfort and nurturance. A dried fig from my food pouch, split open and slid up her willow legs, became her vagina and pelvis, a symbol of sex and fertility. I adorned her with a downy white cockatoo feather, representing the way she enhanced her beauty with attractive clothes.

The doll was remarkably beautiful and I felt proud of my handiwork. I stood her up in the sandy soil and expressed the regret, sorrow, frustration, fear and gratitude I felt towards her. I carried her down to the riverside and stood her between some rocks. Then, as I had in my dream, I ritualistically attempted to dam the river with large rocks. It was obvious that my efforts were pointless.

I could see how much I resisted going with the flow of the river of life and that all of my efforts to hold on to the past were damning my life to hardship and pain. With the medicine doll as my witness, I proclaimed: "I am willing to accept whatever the river of life brings to me."

I turned to the doll, picked her up, gently cradled her in my hands, and thanked her again for all we had shared. I kissed her, said goodbye, and cast her into the current. The gurgling water swiftly carried her away. Deep sobs of grief rose up and out of me. When my tears subsided, I returned to my campsite and burned the debris left from the construction of the doll, symbolically letting go of all the effort I had invested in building our relationship. I walked down to the river and immersed myself, asking that any remaining attachments be washed away.

I spent the remainder of the day watching the river flow by. By evening, I still found myself feeling empty inside. I closed my eyes and the image of the doll came to me. I mentally embraced the image, and it grew within me until it filled my entire body. My emptiness was filled with a sense of my own beauty, strength, creativity and love. All the qualities I had seen in my ex-wife, I was now able to acknowledge in myself.

There were other times in the next several months when my feeling of emptiness would return. At these times I called on the image of the medicine doll, which helped me to regain my sense of wholeness.

The next day, feeling at peace, I followed the stream out of the hills and into the open valley below, where it joined with the road back to Canberra.

*Grey rocks and water below grey skies,*
*Seen through misty windows of grey eyes.*

*Rainy Sunday greys lead me within,*
*Warmth and comfort foster a soft grin.*

*Nothing to do but breakfast in bed,*
*Without the rush, life still moves ahead.*

*Grey quietly sits without the loudness of colour,*
*And humbly finds beauty not known in the other.*

*beauty abounds; remember?*

*there is a light*
*that shines*
*in the darkest*
*and stormiest*
*of days.*

*the fire of death releases the seeds of new life.*

BOONOO BOONOO National Park is located in northeast New South Wales on the upper eastern slopes of the Great Dividing Range. The Boonoo Boonoo River runs through the park and cascades into a deep gorge to form the spectacular Boonoo Boonoo Falls. I had already been fasting two of a planned four day fast, when I traversed the steep trail adjacent to the waterfall. My intention was to cleanse myself of impurities and experience my spiritual essence within this sacred landscape.

Since prehistory, fasting in solitude has been a powerful method of purification and seeking vision. Native Americans, for example, often used this as a "rite of passage" ritual, to facilitate the transition from one stage of life to another; particularly from adolescence to adulthood. [Aboriginal people of Australia when faced with a dilemma or life change might "go walkabout" (a solo journey in the wilderness).]

The youth ventures on his own, away from the comfort, familiarity and security of his family and tribe into the unknowns of the wilderness. He is faced with his weaknesses and fears, both those known to him and those previously unseen, and comes to know courage and other untapped resources. Away from his usual sphere of influence and in the heightened awareness and altered state of consciousness brought on by fasting, he may receive inspiration and a vision of his calling in life. In severing the bond with his family, he discovers a new bond with his inner self and the great spirits of the universe. This bond is forged in the allegorical dramas that unfold during his intimate interactions with Mother Nature.

In Western society, few of us experience rites of passage with this sort of power. We grow up under the influence of our particular familial and ethnic beliefs. We are taught how others want us to behave, think and feel, so we might best fit into the existing framework of our family and society. In most cases we are not taught to question or seek understanding of ourselves. Instead we follow the maps of our social conditioning, continuing along the prescribed path, until we find ourselves so lost or in pain, that we are forced to question or continue suffering. These crises come in the form of divorce, drug/alcohol abuse, unfulfilling careers, loneliness and isolation, as well as, a myriad of emotional and psychological disorders. Isn't it a shame we often don't come to this brink of desperation and introspection until we are in the throes of a mid-life crisis? By this time, many of us have already passed on to our children these same types of unquestioning, uninspired attitudes.

Descending the steep palisade was a difficult passage. Hot and sweaty, I stopped at the base of the crashing falls to cool off in the misty air. Having not eaten, I wasn't walking at my usual robust pace, and meandered slowly down through the gorge alongside the stream. I stopped often to reflect on the changing vistas and my passing thoughts. Later that afternoon, I exited the national park noticing the obvious markings of cattle along the way. I saw no people or cattle. The valley had widened into gentle sloping hills of eucalyptus.

As the afternoon shadows lengthened, I began looking for a place of power to make camp. I sat and stood in different spots to find one that felt right. Finally, as the sun hovered over the western ridge, I walked down to the river for a drink. I sat on a smooth sun-warmed boulder mindlessly listening to the sounds of cascading water. My eyes rested in the comfort of billowy clouds that drifted overhead in a sea of deep blue. Intuitively, I stood, turned and climbed over a small bank of rock, where I found a flat sand bar perfect for my tent. My inner voice said, "This is it".

After setting up my tent, my mind in its habitual way gravitated towards food. "Instead of the ritual of an evening meal," I said aloud, "let me find sustenance in the richness of the setting sun." I walked up the eastern hillside above the shadow cast by the opposite ridge, into the waning sunlight.

A promiment rise between two fire singed trees beckoned me. Upon a rock pedestal, I faced the sun with closed eyes, my inner landscape was illuminated with orange light.

I prayed to the setting sun for help in finding harmony and balance in my life. Standing motionless for quite some time, my awareness gradually settled into my body. I noticed different areas of tension and let them go. The orange light shimmered before my eyes, and encircled me like a cocoon. My awareness melted into the warm glow. A sound in the grass caught my attention and I opened my eyes to see a juvenile wallaby bounding across the hillside. The rise and fall of my breathing coincided with his hops. As the wallaby merged into the darkened forest, I was surprised that the sun had been down for some time.

I gazed across the valley. With almost imperceptible movement, I meditatively swayed from side to side. I slid easily to my left, but moving to the right was like pushing through mud. A dull ache became noticeable in my right hip and I felt an empty coldness in my waist above it. I shifted my weight slightly to ease the discomfort, with no effect. I knew I was holding some old pain, but I said to myself, "Not now, I'll deal with it later." With shaky legs and a chill on my spine, I gathered some firewood on my way back to camp.

Later in the evening, I sat warming my back and I stared into the darkness of a moonless night. I felt empty in my abdomen. My thoughts went first to food, then to a cup of herb tea. I have often tried to appease this feeling by eating, but since it usually has nothing to do with hunger, I end up stuffing myself mindlessly. I sat with my emptiness and stared hypnotically into the black forest. My trance took me back in time.

I was a young boy looking longingly at my mother in the kitchen. I went to her; when she tried to comfort me, I backed off and pushed her away. My unspoken cry was, "I don't want you!" She offered me a homemade cookie, which I ate, and then asked for another. She said, "Okay, but no more. You've had enough."

I responded angrily, she tried to comfort me and again I pushed her away. My unspoken words this time were, "You're not the one I want!" A pain deep in my gut began to well up, moving into my chest, then my throat and finally erupting, "I want my Daddy! . . . Daddy, Daddy, where are you? Where are you when I need you?" I broke into deep sobbing, my tears flowed freely. My sobs wrenched into convulsions and dry heaves, my body wanting to expel all the junk I'd eaten to stuff my feelings down. With an outpouring of yellow bile, my sorrow turned to rage. "I hate you!" Then my childhood oath spewed forth, "If you don't want me, I won't want you!" The pain of cutting off from my own emotional needs flooded through and then gradually subsided. I added more wood to the glowing embers and rolled onto my back.

Gazing into the black starless sky. The little boy in me asked, "Are you up there God?" I remembered going to church; God seemed so distant and unapproachable. He was an unknowable father figure who looked after us, allotting awards and punishments accordingly. Much the same as the role my father played in our family.

Fathers have become increasingly more distant from their families. Since the Industrial Revolution they no longer worked in and around the home, where children could share in their labours. Instead they went off to factories and businesses, returning in the evening tired and unavailable for the most part, to their children. I remember my mother saying: "Leave your father alone, he's had a hard day at work."

In fathers' absence, children have become increasingly dependent on their mothers, who try hard, but can't adequately fulfil both roles. Coincidentally, during this period of time, God and spirituality, has become more removed from our daily rituals, replaced by an insatiable hunger for *things* to gratify and comfort us. Which not only leads us further from God, but has driven us to exhaust mother earth's limited resources, creating tragic imbalances in the environment.

In my solitude and emptiness, I acknowledged my need to seek fulfilment in Father essence — spirit, transcendence, wisdom, creativity — and find a more balanced relationship to Mother essence — physical nuturance and pleasure, security, comfort. Tribal cultures living closer to nature, free of materialistic trappings have emphasized communing with the spirit world. They have prayed, sung, chanted, danced, meditated, and fasted to offer thanks, seek direction and understanding, and to celebrate their relationship with the natural environment and the creative force of the universe. How barren my life has been of such meaningful rituals. I asked God, as the creative, guiding force of the universe, to guide me to a new understanding and connection with him, and to help me to find rituals that enable me to live a more spiritually meaningful life.

Late into the early hours of the morning I sat by the fire. Ceremoniously, I placed one twig at a time on the fire, each one representing the beliefs that isolate me from: other people, God, Mother Earth and the universe as a whole. Some of these beliefs I was able to identify; others I left to my unconscious mind and the forces of the universe to sort out, or to bring into my awareness at the appropriate time.

When the wood ran out, I laid down in my sleeping bag. The sky had cleared, revealing endless dots of illumination. I gazed beyond the earth for a long time, feeling more at one with existence. I didn't remember falling asleep, but woke up early to a grey sky, feeling rested despite having little sleep. After sitting for a long time watching the stream flow by, I jumped into the cold bracing river, forcing deep breaths into my lungs. Feeling invigorated I set off to explore more of the region back upstream.

I came to a junction of a small creek, and sheltered my pack between some boulders. Facing into the unexplored valley, I asked to be guided to a place of power and to access the unknown or forgotten in me. The valley quickly narrowed into a steep ravine and the tiny creek disappeared underground. I followed a smaller dry creek-bed up to my right, which cut into the steep hillside. I felt very sluggish, as if layers of heavy cloaks were weighing me down. Brought to a halt, an inner voice nagged at me: "This is leading you nowhere. There's no magic here, why don't you just head back!"

Something in my heart urged me on. A large newly fallen tree lay in my path. Down on all fours, I squeezed through a tight passage between the branches and under the trunk. Crawling uphill, I felt like those same heavy cloaks were hanging me up on the tree limbs. "What are you doing crawling around out here like an animal!" the critical voice barked. A fierceness from within, exploded me out of that stuck place and I found myself clambering up the hillside like a madman, or was it a wildman? I was panting and snorting. My eyes opened wide, scanned the hillside, bouncing around in their sockets. I wasn't looking to see what there was to see; nor was I thinking about it or labelling my experience. My eyes were just following some instinctive chaotic pattern of scanning, taking in my entire surroundings, without placing any importance or focussing on any one thing.

My body was moving with power and grace. Pausing briefly on the hillside, my head and eyes continued to scan. Breaths were full and deep, impassioned with a chesty growl. I felt feral and free. Further up the steep gully I reached two monumental rocks standing in tandem, forming a giant altar and marking the source of this watercourse. I paused for a moment in reverence at the base, then circled around to find a perch on top that overlooked the wooded valley.

My body was vibrating with aliveness, energy flowed through me into the ground and up through the ground into me. My fingers energetically extended out to touch my surroundings. I heard birds squawking their calls off to my right.

"What's my call?" I asked. "I am free," my voice resonated. "I am free to be me!" I yelled a bit louder. Then: "I am free! . . . I am free to be me!" Over and over, louder and louder, again and again, in a rhythmic chant, like a Negro spiritual — rich, soulful and full of passion. I sang my heart out to the world and in turn I was filled with ecstasy. Tears of joy streamed down my face. I felt like I was reunited with a long lost friend.

As the song ended, the rhythm in my limbs amplified into a cathartic dance. Uninhibited, I flew in circles around the top of the altar. Normally I might have been more careful, but with complete presence of mind and body, I was fearless. My dance was innately connected to those rocks, the earth, the sky and the trees around me.

The dance eventually subsided. I sat in a long grateful silence. The rest of the afternoon was spent meandering, prancing and gliding through the forest and hillsides, finishing with a swim in the creek. I slept deep and long that night.

The next day, before beginning my hike out of the park and the ending of my fast, I reflected on my experiences and revelations of this quest. I asked the guiding forces of the universe to help me to incorporate this age old instinctual wisdom into my life. I had a cup of tea and a small bowl of porridge, and then began my return hike.

*Life's a revealing stroll along destiny's stream.*
*The river's course is set, although I choose my own path.*
*Still, I stay within the channel of her calling.*

*My walk of life may be quick, slow, hassled or calm.*
*Still the river flows on, over rocks and through pools,*
*Sharing passage with converging tributaries.*

*At times my choices take me bouncing on boulders,*
*Crunching on sandy banks, sliding through moistened grass,*
*Or rolling in the laughter of gurgling falls.*

*Then I find myself struggling*
*through stubborn brush,*
*Snagging on thorny vines,*
*slipping on rocky slime,*
*Or inching along ledges to*
*abrupt impasses.*

*Stuck in muddy indecision's dark*
*sinking grip,*
*There is no right way to tread,*
*there is no wrong way,*
*Yet sometimes I must backtrack*
*and find a new way.*

*Whichever path I choose and*
*wherever I am,*
*I can be lost on false trails of*
*future or past,*
*When the glimmer of beauty's*
*recognition*
*Reveals my location in the*
*eternal now.*

*the river of life carries us to places of magnificence and grace,*
*where following our true course requires a leap of faith.*

In the shade of towering
companions,
Calm eddy lives in swirling
acceptance.
Swimming in the grace of
river strong.

The ever jubilant falls
above
Fill her with soft bubbling
excitement
Which keeps her dancing
in frothy lace.

Fleeting voyagers from all
about
Blend into a prismatic
collage,
Forming her sphere of
relationships

Some harbour for a month
or a day,
Before continuing on their
way.
While one may stay and
sink to her depths.

After floods when all is
washed away,
Her empty solitude is still
filled
By a deep undercurrent of
love.

In her wholeness she
patiently waits
With the knowledge that
all she needs and
wants
Is already flowing towards
her in time.

*humans are the only creatures capable of lying.*
*Our greatest lies are the ones told to convince ourselves what isn't in our best interests; is.*

DAINTREE NATIONAL PARK in northern Queensland, is the gateway to the relatively unspoiled natural environment of the Cape York Peninsula. In 1984, this area was brought to the awareness of most Australians, when environmental groups protested a road being cut through the rainforest. Although it has opened the Cape Tribulation area to tourism, the road is already in danger of eroding and the silt that runs off this hillside scar is damaging the reef and marine life in the sea below.

I entered the southern end of the Daintree at Mossman Gorge, and made my way up river from there. The hillsides were densely woven with rainforest vegetation (this area is home to some 1160 species of higher plants and trees and 214 species of ferns). When I tried to find my way into the forest I was snagged by wait-a-while vines. No sooner would I escape from one, when I'd feel the bite of another into my skin or clothing.

"Better to keep to the river bed," I decided. When it rains, this steep channel floods quickly. But it hadn't rained for a while, so the water level was low enough to clamber over and between the massive boulders of this maze-like obstacle course. The going was slow, but each difficult climb led me into the presence of unique cascade filled pools, that reflected the canopy of exotic hardwood trees and drooping vines. Black Cockatoos, Rainbow Lorikeets and myriads of unidentified birds glided through the opening in the forest above the river, calling out from the tree tops. Small tree frogs shyly watched me from mossy tree trunk perches and the under-side of lush leaves. A rainforest dragon lizard slipped hastily into a protected pool as I slid down the rounded side of a granite boulder.

I'd pause to reflect on the beauty, take a photo or have a swim, but kept mostly on the move. Later in the afternoon I began looking for a campsite. The sky was heavy with clouds, so I thought it was best to camp above the river, in case of flooding. The river valley was very steep and still impenetrable, confining me to the river bed. Finally, a tributary creek offered me a patch of sand next to what might become a small raging torrent, rather than the possible path of a tidal wave of raging rainfall runoff.

While gathering firewood, I found a number of black bean seed pods, each pod contained three chestnut-like seeds. They looked edible, so I threw six hulled nuts into the fire to add to my otherwise bland dinner. After letting them roast for about an hour, I tenuously tasted my first black bean nut. It was delicious so I ate four more.

The night was comfortably warm. After dinner I ambled up the steep embankment and watched my camp-fire slowly die. Sitting on the slope, I was engulfed in darkness. The shroud of cloud cover and the veil of foliage overhead, kept even the faintest glimmer of star light from reaching my retina. Once my pupils opened wide enough, a faint aura emanating from the trees gave me a hint of their whereabouts.

As my mind eased, rustling activity on the leafy forest floor, scratching and picking on a tree trunk, the delicate gurgling of the creek and a mouse-like squeak, all amplified. I stared into the darkness that embraced me, and the empty blackness filled my inner being. My body merged with the mountain as my vision sank into a black inland sea.

"Am I dying?" I thought. I felt as though I was disappearing. However, my desire to go into the void overpowered my anxiety and my awareness returned to the expanding realm of the unknowable.

I don't know how long I sat there, because my time conscious mind had dissolved. I was only vaguely aware of the rise and fall of my breath and the tranquil movements hidden in the night, which were like the shoreline and subtle landscape surrounding the bottomless lake I floated in. I forgot if my eyes were open or closed, I just drifted.

A faint voice from a distant shore called out, "That's far enough Eric. Come back. It's time to return now."

My awareness slowly swam back towards the faint shapes and vivid sounds of the forest. I grasped a fist full of decaying leaves, their musty aroma pulled me ashore, and I reoriented myself to solid ground.

I felt my way back to camp. After a few hours of resting in peace, nightmarish visions of isolation and death began to haunt me. Finally a painful pressure in my abdomen forced me out of my fitful slumber. My belly had blown up like a balloon. I realised it must have been those black bean nuts I had eaten.

"Oh no, I've done it now," I thought. I've poisoned myself trying to be the Bush Tucker Man. What a stupid way to die. Maybe I can walk back to the campground and someone can take me to the hospital."

"No that won't work, it will only help the poison travel through your body faster," another voice responded.

"Hold on!" the more rational part of my mind said, "You're not dead yet and it's too dark to go anywhere right now anyway."

My belly was continuing to expand and I desperately needed to release the pressure. I began massaging my belly to loosen things up, hoping I could squeeze something out. Nothing came.

"I'm going to explode," I thought. I felt like a balloon that was perilously reaching its bursting point with each molecule of breath blown into it.

I stood up and walked around a bit to relieve the pressure, still nothing. I squatted. Finally a couple of gurgles and pops shifted the pressure. I took a deep breath and pushed. The tiniest little fart squeaked out. Not very satisfying, but it was something. I stood up and then squatted again. This time a nice trumpet of pungent air came streaming forth. Relief, then, after a deep rumbling in my guts, my belly swelled up even larger than before.

"I'm generating gas more quickly than I can get rid of it," I thought, I envisioned the headline, HIKER KILLED BY GIANT FART. I laughed, but really I was scared shitless. I screamed out in pain and fear. Another burst of putrid gas escaped. It smelled like a dead animal.

A haunting vision of the empty eyes of a dead deer I had found years before made me shudder. I had looked into those eyes and for the first time in my life had felt how close death was at all times.

So much of the time, I live my life as if I'll be young forever. I put off doing the things I need to do. I cling to my addictions and self destructive habits, telling myself, "I'll give them up soon, my body can handle it." Every time I deny what I know is best for me and what I really want, I take a step toward sickness and death, away from health and life.

We are doing the same thing with our planet. We contaminate, pollute and destroy, thinking the planet can take it, but this is no longer the case. We may have reached the point of no return. Or maybe like the alcoholic who finally has hit rock bottom, we will come face to face with our death and just before it's too late, surrender to our higher wisdom and heal ourselves and our planet.

A big fart escaped my bowels and I felt relieved. But when I stood up, my legs were trembling. A nauseous blanket of cold sweat enveloped me.

"If this is my death, I am going to face it standing," I decided. My whole body was shaking. A series of heaves wracked my guts and throat. I doubled over in pain and started shaking uncontrollably, but my feet remained rooted to the earth.

"I won't die, you asshole," I screamed. I shook my fists and stomped my feet in defiance of death. Another dry retch and my defiance was broken.

"I promise I'll never eat junk food or drink beer again," I pleaded.

"Oh, really?" another thought interjected.

"What do you want from me?"

"Let go."

Another fart came, I let my weight sink into my ankles and my whole body began waving spasmodically. As the subtle illumination of dawn filtered through the trees, I let myself approach the black void that invited me from within. Letting go of the fear I held in my anus and the gas dammed up behind it, I closed my eyes and entered the darkness.

I sank to my knees and into the emptiness. I lay prostrate on the ground and in my surrender, found peace.

"I'm ready to die now," I murmured. Blissful weeping melted my aches. Lying in a pool of tears. I knew that I would live, although an old fearful part of me had died.

I felt a rumbling in my bowels again, but it wasn't a fart. Hastily I staggered away from my campsite and dug a hole. I squatted, and out poured a deluge of diarrhoea. I felt drained and empty. I buried the remains and retreated to my bed. I laid motionless watching and listening to the forest awaken. Exhaustion delicately tugged at my eyelids and the deep rhythm of my breathing lulled me asleep.

For a long time after waking, I laid in the embrace of the hard ground which comforted me. In the afternoon, I explored further up the creek, then ended the day down by the Mossman River, swimming and jumping off boulders. When evening descended, I sought sanctuary in the smoky light of the campfire. My stomach shunned even the idea of food. I sat on the periphery of the emptiness inside my belly, not wanting to get too close. Still drained from my ordeal, I fell asleep early.

I was awakened by raindrops dripping from dimly lit leaves. I packed up camp quickly. My strength had nearly returned and I decided to head back to town. After one near death experience, I didn't want to take any chances with the flood waters of a tropical storm. Retracing my path of two days before, and going down hill quickened the pace. I moved with urgency, but had great fun ruining my pants sliding down the smooth surface of the river boulders.

Sometimes I feel I'm keeping just a few steps ahead of my anxiety. I keep myself busy with my compulsions and addictions to avoid facing myself. On this day I felt no such anxiety, I had faced my fear of death and lived. What was there to run from?

*harmony is composed of life's contradictions existing side by side.*

• • • • •

IT WAS AUGUST when I reached the south coast of Western Australia. After several cold, rainy winter days, the sun burst through, and I leapt at the opportunity to hike through the Nuyts Wilderness and adjoining Walpole-Nornalup National Park.

The worn path began in a grove of Karri trees and I followed it down along a small creek and through a thicket of wattles. After a short stop at the beach nestled in the small cove at the bottom of the trail, I trekked westward on a well-marked trail that traversed the granite headlands. Soon the trail disappeared into the heath-clad slopes. I pushed my way through this dense growth which, at the best of times, surrounded my knees, while at other times, had me crawling on all fours under tangled growth. Throughout the afternoon, showers kept the bushes damp. They in turn dried themselves on my clothing.

The rain fell between the patches of blue sky and were accompanied by sparkling rainbows that rose from and fell into the white capped ocean. I could feel a storm brewing, and pushed on into a steady southerly wind to find a campsite.

All afternoon I had been walking atop perilous cliffs. I finally reached a ravine where I could make camp on the crest of a small sand dune. This was the only feasible tent site I had seen in hours. It didn't offer much shelter from the driving wind, but it was home for the night. The tent stakes wouldn't hold in the sand so I anchored the tent with sticks and rocks. I had just taken refuge in the tent when the sky exploded with a torrent of rain. The wind accelerated to over 60 km/hour on its way through the ravine. I managed to get a candle lit, but the tent, expanding and contracting like an accordion, extinguished the flame.

Sitting in the dark I was overcome by fears. "What if my tent is ripped apart and I'm forced to wait out the storm in the cold wet night?" I imagined my parents, after months of not hearing from me, begin to ask questions, not knowing my body had been washed into the sea.

Instead of being consumed by fears, I decided to enjoy this harrowing experience, much like I would a roller coaster ride. I reminded myself to keep breathing deeply when I thought the tent poles might break, and howled back at the wind when I thought it might rip my thin layer of nylon protection wide open. My make-shift tent stakes were being pulled loose from their tenuous holds in the sand, so every 15-20 minutes I was running out of the tent naked to replace them. This added to the humour of the situation. After a couple of hours I realized I was safe, and fell asleep emotionally drained.

In the morning the sun peeked through the clouds, lighting up the water-glazed granite formations I had climbed on. I felt agitated inside and wasn't able to relax and enjoy the beautiful vistas. A voice harangued at me: "This place isn't so great, get going, there's something better somewhere else." Then I thought: "What is really going on?" My eyes were so sensitive to the light that I could hardly look past my nose.

I sat down and stared painfully at the waves breaking on the rocks. I took some deep breaths, and tears came to my eyes. I was soon sobbing, acknowledging how frightened I was. The evening before had touched deep fears about opening up, trusting life, and living to my fullest capacity. I realized how I use my judgments and criticisms of people or situations to avoid looking within. After my tears subsided, my eyes opened to all the beauty that danced around me. I sat in peaceful wonder, gazing at the seascape that was perpetually alive with motion. When I did move on, it wasn't out of fear, instead I was drawn forward by curiosity and enthusiasm for what lay ahead.

Eyes full of judgement that say this coast's not so great,
Squint in recoil from a morning not so bright.

Feet quick to run off, in a quest for new beauty,
Wanting to escape unrecognised discomfort.

A moment's hesitation decides to hold ground,
To face overcast skies and turbulent waters.

Surging breath begins riding on tidal-like swells,
Rising and falling between hard rocks of holding.

The squinting cracks etched in dull eyes'
granite temples
Rigidly cling to doubtfulness and denial.

In come sobbing waves of simple
acknowledgement,
Bringing accepting tears to warm
softening cheeks.

Peace cascades awareness back in
wide-eyed wonder
To the oneness, power and
beauty of the sea.

*Walking on the solid ground of conceptions,*
*Expanding horizons stretch all directions,*

*Exploring the range of possibilities,*
*Arriving at the brink of sensibilities,*

*Leaping in faith to oceanic oneness,*
*Inconceivable miracles call on us.*

*Coasting down to the seashore on a notion,*
*Soothing cloud cover excludes sunscreen lotion,*

*Swelling wind-driven tides set waves in motion,*
*Flooding overcast pools with commotion,*

*Gusting sea mists concoct a magic potion,*
*Stirring my heart with ecstatic emotion,*

*Spontaneously displaying devotion,*
*I dance on the edge of earth, sky and ocean.*

*The search for understanding is unending.*
*The discovery of appreciation is instantaneous.*

WHILE STILL in California, one of my friends asked if I was going to Monkee Mia to see the dolphins. I had never heard of it and although her description sounded interesting, I wasn't making any promises. While in Hawaii someone asked me the same thing, but again I wasn't sure if it was worth the long trip to the far northwest of the continent. After arriving in Sydney someone asked me again; still I wouldn't make a commitment.

I stayed three weeks in Melbourne. One day, while exploring the city on a bicycle, I felt irresistibly drawn down one particular street, around a corner, and right to a bookshop specializing in women's books. I walked in and directly approached the first and only book I saw — *The Dolphins' Gift* by Elizabeth Gawain.

I read for over an hour, when the shopkeeper asked me if there was something I wanted to buy. Still resisting all the omens, I said "No."

That evening, talking casually with a friend, I felt a shiver go up my spine. He said he had a friend in Denham, the nearest town to Monkee Mia, and that I should visit him. Still unsure, I took the address just in case.

Finally, browsing through a bookshop in Darwin, *The Dolphins' Gift* was on sale for half price, and, being a sucker for a bargain, I decided to answer all the signs pointing to Monkee Mia.

Monkee Mia is located approximately 800 kilometres north of Perth in Shark Bay. The outer boundary of the bay, Steep Point, is the western-most point of the Australian continent. As early as 1964, dolphins have been swimming into the shallow waters of the beach here to make contact with humans. There is a small caravan park which attracts fishermen and dolphin lovers.

It was midday when I arrived. The tour buses had also arrived and people of all ages were interacting with the dolphins, who seemed to have an uplifting effect on everyone. One older man, arms crossed and carrying a bitter grimace on his face, escorted his children to the water's edge. He barked commands at them. But then something wonderful happened as he watched the dolphins play with his children. His face relaxed, his arms unlocked, and slowly a smile started infiltrating the fortress of his down turned mouth, then it radiated outward until it had conquered his entire deeply lined face.

I felt like a shy teenager at a school dance. The dolphins were the pretty girls, and I was the insecure loner, standing off to the side, not knowing how to approach them. I was frightened they wouldn't have the same special feeling towards me.

People were feeding them fish sold by the park rangers, so I did the same. Again, adolescent feelings of jealousy surfaced as I watched others flirt and mingle so freely. I wanted the dolphins to give *me* attention, not because I had fish but because they thought I was special.

I offered a fish to a dolphin (named Joy, I was told), and as she took it from me, she nipped the end of my finger, drawing blood. My teenage nightmare had come true. I felt hurt and rejected. Joy looked directly at me with one penetrating eye underlined by her permanent smile. I felt she was trying to say something to me, but in my muddled state I couldn't understand what it was. Standing knee deep in the water, I watched the children playing so freely with them and wished I could do the same, but I seemed to have erected a barrier between me and everyone else, dolphins and humans alike.

I decided to find a campsite and return later. I was so broke that I couldn't afford the camping fee, so I walked down the coastline and found an illegal site hidden in the bush. I felt guilty about breaking the rules, but I was happy to have the peace and quiet.

I wrote in my journal to sort out my feelings and the events of the day. I couldn't understand why these peaceful beings would bite me without any provocation on my part. Was there a difference between me and the children who played so freely and effortlessly with the dolphins? After some inner searching, I realized that I had approached them with expectations. Not only hoping I would be treated as special but also expecting to be rejected. In a sense, I got exactly what I was asking for.

Near sunset I went back down to the beach. Two dolphins were playing with a young man and woman. I wanted to make contact, but I held back. Finally, in the reddish glow of dusk, I waded into the water about fifteen metres from where the four of them played. A few moments later the dolphins turned and swam out to sea. My heart sank, but I thought, "See you tomorrow," and headed back to my campsite.

The next morning I decided to pretend that I had never read *The Dolphins' Gift*. I would approach them without any idea of what should happen. I know I've often tried to hide my insecurity and ignorance behind the mask of being a know-it-all, and thus rob myself of the experience of learning.

There were three dolphins, the park ranger, and one other person, when I arrived. I observed their interaction before I entered the water.

Then I waded in and held my hand out, as a dolphin glided by. Slowly, I warmed to them. But if one would swim away to play with one of the others, I would feel a little rejected. "It's okay," I told myself. "They're just loving everyone equally."

After a while Joy swam into the gathering, greeting the others. I felt anxious about making contact with her. She swam past the woman on my left and then next to me. I reached down and stroked her smooth rubbery skin. She circled around my knees and then drifted on her side towards the open water. She looked coyly at me with the eye that was out of the water. I wanted to ask her why she had bitten me yesterday, but I realized it really didn't matter.

One of the other dolphins came around to visit me. I gave him a hug and instinctively told him how wonderful he was. I felt a rush of love for him and all the dolphins, which then spilled over to everyone there. Joy returned but I still felt a bit uncomfortable with her. She brushed up against me, swam past and then back again.

"Are you trying to tell my something?" I asked her silently.

"Forgive yourself," echoed in my mind.

"What's that supposed to mean?" I replied.

I watched Joy and the other dolphins exchange affection with the humans. Neither the dolphins nor the people were doing anything special to earn love or to be loved. I became aware of the pressure I put on myself to be special — by being smart or clever or whatever — to earn the love of others. I wanted to love and to feel love unconditionally. I decided that I really didn't have much experience with this and I would let the dolphins teach me.

Joy swam back in my direction. I knew she had never felt any malice towards me, it had only been self-doubt that caused me to see the bite as rejection. It was an accident, or the result of not exercising enough caution when feeding her. She nudged a piece of sea grass in my direction, I waved it in front of her and ran in the shallows as she chased after me. I was giggling like a three-year-old.

I spent the next hour frolicking with the dolphins. My heart lightened. That afternoon I went for a long walk down the beach. At sunset, I walked out on the sandy shelf that was exposed by the

low tide. The violets and pinks were beautifully reflected in the tide pools and puddles. I felt thankful for the events of the day and to be graced with such beauty. I thought about the older gentleman I had seen on the first day. He was really a reflection of myself and how I had been feeling. I immediately felt love for him, and I knew that I had forgiven myself.

I spent the next four days playing with dolphins, chatting with humans, and exploring the long stretches of beach and adjoining bushland. Joy and I became good friends. I found myself being less analytical and judgemental, and more comfortable experiencing the "joy" of living.

*to fight nature is a lost cause.*
*Eventually balance will be restored,*
*even if it means unconditional surrender.*

*Sharp grass covers round mountains.*
*Scratchy brush dots red rock spines.*
*Rugged iron-forged beauty*
*Seems unfriendly in nature.*

*A windy rust dusty road,*
*Scraped in, around and over,*
*Carries curious seekers*
*To marvellous new vistas.*

*All those who have ventured here*
*Walk the slim path to the edge.*
*Some remain on the lookout,*
*Careful not to get too close.*

*Their footholds feel insecure.*
*Inside they fear they might fall.*
*The rule is look but don't touch,*
*Like a souvenir shop stop.*

*There are those who aren't afraid.*
*Doubtless they walk on the edge*
*Feeling a yearning inside*
*Urging them to go deeper.*

*The unworn pathway's not long,*
*Although it's rocky and steep.*
*Requiring care and patience*
*When wanting to venture deep.*

*When exploring the canyon,*
*They're bound to follow the flow,*
*Discovering perspectives,*
*Others don't see when aloof.*

*The fine work is polished,*
*Just room for one at a time,*
*Through cavern-like passageways*
*That are glowing from above.*

*It is here, deep in the heart*
*Where the real magic awaits,*
*In these great red rock canyons*
*And with all friends that we make.*

*to dominate,*
*control*
*or exploit*
*is a sure sign*
*of low self worth.*
*Respect yourself,*
*respect one another,*
*respect the planet.*

THE FITZROY RIVER winds its way 1000 kilometres from its sources to the King Sound and Indian Ocean of Australia's northwest. Approximately 300 kilometres from the sea it passes through a huge limestone wall. This wall was created 350 million years ago by coral-like creatures that colonized what was a large barrier reef at that time.

After thousands of years the river has carved a deep channel through the ancient reef, known as Geike Gorge. The fossilized remains of sea creatures share their home with living sharks, sawfish, and stingrays. These ocean-dwelling animals somehow found a way to adapt to fresh water when the ocean last receded.

I arrived at Geike Gorge in the late afternoon. I jogged upstream along the sandy river bank as the sun descended. The shadow cast by the western canyon rim crept layer by sedimentary layer up the eastern wall. In succession, the tips of the rocky spires burst with light before succumbing to shadow.

Half an hour later, I slid down a steep sand bank, picked my way through the river willows and set up my camera on the river's edge. I was intent on getting a good photograph of the gorge in the fading light. A light breeze blew over the river and I worried that it would prevent a good reflection. Meanwhile, my mind was preoccupied: "What am I going to have for dinner? Am I in the best place for the photo? What am I doing tomorrow?"

In a moment's reflection, I clearly saw how my preoccupations blinded me to the beauty of this passing instant. I focused my muddled attention on the rippled surface of the river and watched my breathing become deeper and more rhythmical. My mind and the water's surface settled in unison. The grey rock reflected in the river came alive with radiant colour. Tingling shivers straightened my spine, leaving goose bumps on my arms. Internally, I celebrated the joy of witnessing my oneness with nature. I identified with a deep part of me — the silent observer of my thoughts, feelings, body sensations and perceptions — and felt blessed by such pure awareness.

Just after the glow reached its peak, a relentless sense of purpose pulled me out of my reverie in time to take a photo. The tropical dusk gave way to starlight, and a faint sliver of moon afforded me just enough light to find my way back to camp.

The following morning, in predawn darkness, I slipped quietly out of camp, quickly retracing my steps of the previous evening. As light crept into the eastern sky, I climbed a jagged limestone bluff above the river. Staring into the water, I watched reflected clouds turn violet, pink and then gold as the earth rolled over to greet the sun.

Something weighed on my heart. It was a glorious morning but a constriction around my chest made it difficult to breathe in the beauty. I had no conscious awareness of anything bothering me. I leaned back over a rounded boulder so my arms and chest opened wide. I breathed into the tightness, with progressively deeper breaths. A demanding sense of inertia pleaded with me to remain contracted. Although tempted, a lust for freedom carried me on. There were a few clicks and clunks as my spine chiropractically adjusted itself. My breathing became fuller, more pleasurable. The rhythm steadily increased with each exhalation. My whole body tingled. Three guttural groans released a knot in my diaphragm, sending an orgasmic pulse of warmth flooding through my guts and down my legs to my feet. My breath slowly calmed to where it was barely perceivable. I felt as though I was floating on a calm pool, slowly drifting and rotating, watching my inner sky circle above me. For an eternal instant I felt drawn into

*Streams of thought cut deep into landscapes of living*
*Etching and carving the perceptions of being.*

*Only when the stream is calm and serene,*
*Can true reflections and wisdom be seen.*

a keyhole of light shining in the centre of my mind's eye. The moment I merged with the light it was gone, but I knew that light was me and that was all that really mattered. An image of a large hawk seemed to escape through an unseen door in my rib cage. It soared skyward, taking my awareness with it. Flying towards the clouds, I remembered myself lying on the rock staring wide-eyed into the sky. Then the hawk was gone.

"Wow!" I exclaimed. "That was pretty interesting."

The hard stone seemed to be increasing its pressure on the base of my skull, into my middle back, my calves and heels. I felt welded in place and was mildly surprised when I was able to slowly turn my head and see something other than sky. The rest of my body followed my head and eventually found its way upright. I felt no older than two. My surroundings seemed so awesome, I felt so little

and naive. As I stood, I felt like a new born foal standing on wobbly legs. Birds I hadn't noticed before filled my ears with a symphony of songs. The plants, trees, rocks and water looked so alive. Even the long shadows that hid behind rocky knobs seemed to breathe. I tenderly walked to the edge of the steep cliff, sat down and dangled my legs over the side. Swinging them from side to side, tears welled up in my eyes. I grieved for the little boy in me. So much of the time I shut him away in a dark hidden room, making the excuse that, "I'm too busy trying to accomplish something."

The little boy in me said, "Quit trying so hard, it's all right not to always have a purpose to your actions. Just relax and let yourself be."

I lectured myself, "You've been on holiday long enough and it's time to get serious again." Deep inside, I knew freeing myself from self-limiting concepts was the work I most needed to do. Nothing was more important.

I recalled an idea I'd conceived six months previously — after feeling anxious about not doing anything "productive", I recognized I was beginning a nine-month gestation period within the womb of Mother Nature. This was a time to be nourished and grow internally, so that I could be reborn into a new concept of myself, with the opportunity to make new choices in how I wanted to live my life. I left my mother's womb after less than eight months, and then, for much of my life, continued with the pattern of pushing myself into things before I was ready. This time I wanted to stay in the womb full-term and only re-emerge when I had outgrown the confines of this existence and was ready to move on.

I toddled my way back to camp, meandering between the river bank and the rocky cliffs. I skipped rocks on the glassy river and peaked into nooks and crannies in the limestone walls. While singing choruses in answer to the birds overhead, I suddenly realized how hungry I was and ran the rest of the way back to camp for a hearty breakfast.

*Dare to blaze your own trail.*
*Be humble and wise enough to follow in others' footsteps.*
*But stay alert to when it is time to stray.*
*Follow your heart wherever you go.*

LICHFIELD PARK is approximately 200 km south of Darwin and west of the Stuart Highway. Much of it is undeveloped and only accessible by horseback, four wheel drive, or on foot. The landscape is a mixture of mostly pandanas forest and open meadows. Huge anthill monoliths which often tower as high as four metres stand tall in these open grasslands. A distinctive land formation, "The Lost City" (there are several "lost cities" in secluded spots around Australia) is comprised of a village of large boulders, stacked symmetrically upon one another in avenue-like rows, giving it the appearance of ancient ruins.

Throughout the region, changes in elevation occur abruptly, forming steep escarpments. Thus the various creeks and streams cascade into inspiring waterfalls. Some of the falls I visited were Wangi Falls, Sandy Creek Falls, Surprise Creek Falls, Florence Falls and my favourite, Tolmer Falls.

I approached Tolmer Falls from downstream, walking on the sandy bank of the creek which is cloaked in a narrow strip of rainforest vegetation. Approaching the escarpment, I entered a narrow gorge surrounded by luminescent rose-coloured walls.

After some boulder-hopping, I leaned around a tree and was enchanted by an emerald-green pool set in a large oval amphitheatre. From the open end where I was standing, the falls plunged forty metres into the right corner.

I stripped off my clothes and dived in. I floated under a rainbow mist and played in the effervescent bubbles swirling at the base of the falls. The pounding torrent kept pushing me back, so I circled to the left and crawled onto a small ledge behind the crashing curtain of water.

One segment of the falls was thinner and I thought it would be safe to dive through. I was wrong. It thrust me deep into the churning pool. The current pulled me under, then spat me out into calmer waters. Although the intensity was more than I'd bargained for, I playfully repeated this several times.

To the left of the falls, a large ominous cave beckoned me, I pulled myself out of the water and carefully slithered across the moist rocks of its mouth. Steam hovered over a small pool in the left-hand corner of the dimly lit cavern. Lying down in the warm shallow bath I noticed the vaulted ceiling was decorated with nearly a hundred slumbering bats. The roar of the falls washed through me as I bathed in the warm darkness of this womb-like haven, cleansing me of an accumulated tension.

Emerging from the darkness, I eased myself into the cool emerald water. Silently I glided, my innocent new-born eyes drinking in the serene beauty. I was drawn into a small dark opening in the rock wall. Inside, away from the roar of the outside falls, I heard the sound of more falling water. As my eyes adjusted I discerned a two metre waterfall at the far end of the narrow cave. To my delight, this was also a warm-spring and I luxuriated under the care of its firm pounding massage.

The rest of the day was spent warming in the sun, diving off narrow perches, and resting in the cool shade of the palms. Floating, watching the rock walls circle the luminous sky, I felt immense gratitude for the experience of this paradise. In my reverie, rippling, joyful waves of belly laughs echoed around me.

Then as evening set in, so did the mosquitoes.

I get lost in the advertisement of
urban lights.
Pursuing fantasies of the way
things ought to be.
A calm voice beckons from
the shadows of lonely nights,
But is drowned in the
flooding drone of activity.

Waves slap their sandy knees
in laughter.
Backed by thunderous claps
of amusement and delight.
As I maintain pursuit of those
whims I crave after,
Anxious persistence chases
hopefuls just out of sight.

The endless seeking within
the manufactured maze,
Finally brings me to the city
limits of mind.
In despair I peer beyond the
incandescent haze,
And in my shadow I see a
light that always shines.

In solitude's yawning moment,
I sit by the lilies pondering,
In depth, a pool of galaxies.

Drowning in a fluid universe,
I sense astronomical depths
I am unable to fathom.

Surface tension evaporates,
As I'm quietly submerging
Into astral contemplation.

Adrift within the alpha
waves,
Beyond unchartered inner
space,
Most unlikely to surface are
Meteoric revelations.

Instead, constellations of
growth,
From deep nebulous origins,
Spiral in ascent towards the
light

Navigating me home, on my
Evolutionary voyage.

IN DARWIN I made the acquaintance of Peter, an exceptional photographer who has published two captivating photographic books on the Northern Territory. He asked me to join him on a canoe trip through Katherine Gorge. The Gorge has thirteen sections, separated by rapids. Canoeing upstream, we had to unload our canoe and haul it over the white water and boulders at each transition. Moving upstream, the gorge progressively narrowed. With a little imagination, each section of the vertical landscape displayed ever-changing limestone images of sphinxes, dragons, animals and human faces.

After the second day, we were past the furthest destination of the motorized tour boats that shared the river. The gorge felt different in this atmosphere of solitude. A venerable sacredness surrounded us and I sensed the presence of what might have been nature spirits.

In my experience, nature spirits don't mingle with the masses. And if they did, we're usually too preoccupied with our lives to acknowledge their presence. Occasionally, however, while in nature, we may be overcome by emotions — joy, sadness, anger, fear, love — for which there seems to be no rational explanation.

If we think of nature spirits as energy vortexes, places where the universal life-force is more concentrated or potent (accompanying this power can be intense beauty but often the presence is more subtle), then when we enter this energy field carrying unresolved feelings of anger, fear or grief, they are amplified by this increased charge. The same thing happens when we come in contact with someone who has a powerful affect on us (e.g. a lover, a teacher, a guru). Inhibiting these emotions and preventing the free flow of energy is similar to riding a roller coaster, holding on for dear life, bottling up screams, and feeling miserable. Whereas the person who lets go can enjoy the excitement and even laugh at the fear. With this in mind, these power spots can be tremendous mirrors of our inner state, and give us an opportunity to experience something that goes beyond the usual concepts of ourselves and the world.

One pathway to making contact with nature spirits is through cultivating quiet observation, and waiting. This requires quieting the mind (which is usually more difficult to achieve than not making any noise). Most of our internal chatter is either re-hashing the past or worrying about the future. Both of these preoccupations rob us of the experience of the present. Sometimes I can open all my senses to the world around me. Focusing outward, brings my awareness into the here and now, and lifts me out of the vicious cycles of internal dialogue.

At other times, my anxiety is like a scared little boy who needs attention and reassurance. If I ignore him, he becomes more persistent and annoying. So I patiently listen to his fears and concerns, accept them, but not give them credence or dwell on them. He feels listened to and acknowledged, and curiosity draws his attention away from these concerns to the world that is waiting to be explored. My focus shifts from thoughts, to the silence between thoughts. My ears open to the symphony of sound around me. My eyes adjust to the cinemagraphic dance of light, shadow, colour and movement before me. Opening the pores of my body, I kinesthetically receive the invisible signals transmitted on the airwaves.

In silent observation, my awareness is not searching for stimuli. Rather it is openly receptive to whatever might present itself. It is important to set aside what I think I know and what I expect to find. I must guard my mind against labelling my experience, and wrapping up the infinitely mysterious nature of the universe into a safe box of known entities.

Most of us do this out of fear of the unknown. If we can't explain or control something with our rational minds, then it must be dangerous. In this way, we are like small children who think that

by closing our eyes to something, it won't be there to affect us anymore. This is not more obvious than when we suppress certain thoughts or feelings from our conscious awareness. It is well-known that repressed ideas or feelings usually come back to haunt us in some way (e.g. the person who has repressed the experience of being an abused child becomes involved in abusive relationships as an adult).

In actuality, when we limit our experience of ourselves and the world around us, we fail to recognise and appreciate the greatness of it all. The more we act out of fear, the more we avoid the miraculous beauty, love and strength of all creation, including ourselves.

One afternoon we stopped by a small waterfall that fell into the river. We explored beyond the falls, into the rugged terrain above the narrow gorge. Peter was photographing a lily pond, but my intuition guided me further upstream. I pushed through the tall reeds, crawled under some thick bushes

and came to a grassy bank facing the creek. The black soil filled my nostrils with the damp richness earthworms love. Before me was a calm, enchanting pool.

Gazing into the pool, I sank into a meditative state. I let my awareness sink to the depths of the pool, deepening my own inner peace.

Peter and I made slow, steady progress upstream. By the third night we reached the entrance to the ninth gorge, where a huge rock slide prevented us from going any further by canoe. We returned downstream to a sandy beach and set up camp.

The following day we packed our cameras away. Our intention was to drop the barriers between ourselves and nature's naked power. We reclined on the narrow balconies carved into this chamber of polished rock that thrust skyward out of the reflective emerald water. Glorious mosaic murals decorated the walls of this natural cathedral. We baptised ourselves in the pure holy water, swimming and diving off rocks with child-like abandon. We shared our sanctuary with a variety of birds and even a couple of Johnston Crocodiles (not to be confused with the man-eating Salt Water Crocodiles that inhabit the northern tidal rivers and estuaries).

We climbed beyond the waterfall that marked the river's passage over the massive rock slide, and left each other to be in solitude. I noticed the retreating sun had left the entire canyon to be conquered by shadow, and wondered where the day had gone. Gigantic boulders, burnished from the silty flood waters of the wet season, radiated solar warmth. One boulder magnetically pulled me to its rounded surface. I felt like a baby on his mother's soft warm tummy. As the heat penetrated my body, my flesh melted and merged into the contours of the rock, becoming one with it. I was in a state of being, beyond all doing, at one with my environment, resting in my niche in the river of time. All the small, day-to-day events and changes seemed inconsequential in a time frame of mineral consciousness.

I realized it is from the perspective of eternity that true patience is born. Patience that enables the eternal observer within me to look beyond flooding emotions and stormy life circumstances, to see the perfection within creation's seasonal cycles.

When I finally peeled myself from the rock, my body, like an infant's, was devoid of tension. My skin was stamped with the rock's deep imprints. My skin returned to its previous state, but I carried lasting impressions which I shared with Peter around the campfire that night. Later, we turned our backs to the fire and, in the moonless night, gazed up to the infinite heavens.

"Living in the city," Peter said, "I rarely spend any time gazing at the stars like we are now."

"Me either," I echoed, "I can make the excuse that it's because the city lights drown out the starlight, but honestly it's because I don't take the time."

"It really draws me out of my limited view of myself," he continued, "and I realise how small my problems actually are."

"I know what you mean," I replied. "I think about the earth being just a little spec in a universe of stars and I'm just a spec on the surface of this other spec."

"Yeah, and our lives are just a microsecond in the life of the earth and the earth's life is just a microsecond in the life of the universe," Peter added.

"So what could be so important about the time and money worries I plague myself with?" I said.

"It doesn't make much sense in an infinite universe, does it?"

Day five I spent exploring the eleventh, twelfth and thirteenth gorges. This region was also different from other areas downstream. There were huge piles of driftwood, comprised of everything from tiny twigs to massive tree trunks, resting high above the current water level on rock platforms. They served as monuments to the immense power of this river at the height of the wet season.

I met Peter back at the ninth gorge to capture on film the magic that occurs between the polished rock walls and the fading luminescence of dusk. As the canyon's chiselled features faded into the blackness of night, the desert sky sparked a subtle, amber-rose coloured glow in the faces of the gorge.

These moments, which lie in the crack between night and day, serve as a doorway through which we glimpse a reality beyond our limited perceptions, into a magical and mysterious world, which is always there waiting for us to open our awareness to.

*It's only a rock.*

*If you haven't found what*
*your heart longs for,*
*keep looking.*
*You may never find it.*
*But your search is*
*bound to take you on*
*great adventures to*
*treasures unimagined.*

*to live with thirst,*
*is to realise bliss*
*in a handful of water,*
*and ecstasy*
*in a dreadful downpour.*

*an ageing day gracefully stretches out beside still water.*
*Shadows laid down to rest, reflect memories of his life.*
*His belly's twisted tissues surrender their concern.*
*Awakening a neglected heart with a warm embrace.*

KAKADU NATIONAL PARK is situated on the shores of the Van Dieman Gulf. To the naive observer, this wilderness appears to be uninhabited, untouched by humans (excluding the relatively recent national park developments). But in fact, Kakadu has been home to the Aborigines for over 40,000 years. Their near-zero impact on the environment (especially in contrast to the changes by the Australians of Anglo-European descent), is a tribute to their harmonious relationship with the land.

Although bush fires occur naturally here, the Aborigines burnt the tall grasses and dense undergrowth on a seasonal basis to aid their hunting. Fires may also have served as a means of forest management. Burning the undergrowth early in the dry season creates a cool fire and doesn't permanently damage the trees, whereas fires ignited by electrical storms at the end of the dry season burn hotter, causing far greater damage. After thousands of years, the flora and fauna have adapted to the burning, which has become part of the seasonal cycle.

The most obvious mark left by the native culture are the paintings adorning the caves and protected rock walls along the Arnhem Land Escarpment. These paintings depict events as well as, metaphysical, scientific and cultural perspectives of different historical periods.

The Arnhem Land Escarpment is the most prominent geological formation in the park. This stone-faced cliff marks the boundary between the lowland hills that rise up gradually from the floodplain, and the rugged plateau above. It runs east to west for more than 500 kilometres and climbs to over 200 metres in some places.

I began my exploration at Nourlangie Rock, a gallery of striking paintings. From there I scaled the rocky bluff, walking east on the escarpment until the crevices became too difficult to traverse. So I returned to the shade of the eucalyptus forest at the base of the cliff.

Late June is early in the dry season, but already the small creek beds were parched. The dry season begins in May and ends in October when storm clouds boil into relentless electrical storms. The rainfall, averaging 1400 mm from November to March, spills into the vast catchment area of the plateau and feeds the many river channels before cascading into such spectacular waterfalls as Jimjim, Twin, and U.D.P. Falls.

The run-off flows out of the hills, where without any deep river channels to contain it, it floods the coastal plains, creating a veritable inland sea. This floodplain forms the nucleus of an ecosystem that includes: 1,200 species of plants, 10,000 species of insects, fifty-five species of fish, twenty-five species of frogs, seventy-five species of reptiles, 275 species of birds and fifty-one species of mammals.

Over the low hills, I encountered a dense expanse of spear grass. Silty soil and abundant water had enabled this grass to grow well over my head. My arms and shoulders strained against the golden, spear-like stalks, as I myopically threaded through the mass.

After an hour in this straw maze, I feared being lost and, even more threatening, stumbling across a poisonous snake. To forewarn any legless friends of my presence, I sang songs that would have sent anyone in the opposite direction. Sweaty and drained, I finally emerged into an area recently cleared by fire. Walking easily over the charred whiskers of grass stubble, I understood the important role burning played in flushing out game.

In the open forest my pace quickened, but my limited water supply dwindled sip by sip. I rounded each bend hoping to find a water supply. Then, the last drop was gone. As the afternoon shadows grew longer, my feet began dragging and stumbling over the bone-dry ground. My shoulders ached under the weight of my pack, but my relentless thirst drove me on. Finally, in darkness, I eased into the cool waters of Baraobola Springs to relieve my aching thirst and parched body.

The next morning I watched the sun rise and full moon set from atop the cliffs behind my campsite. From there I followed the narrow gorge to the plateau above, where I swam in a series of clear pools.

Meditating by the river, I focused softly on the bubbles and sparkles. The water gurgled over shaded ebony rocks as the steady shower of sound washed in one ear and out the other, cleansing my mind of its usual chatter. My awareness floated with the passing stream. I could feel currents of energy flowing through my body. These currents swirled around and centred in the area of my umbilicus. All of a sudden, in one motion, a powerful force single-handedly lifted me from my centre to standing. My ears pricked up to the sound of leaves rustling high up in the trees. I followed the sounds, dancing effortlessly over boulders and between trees with the grace of a jaguar. I exercised none of my usual caution in traversing the rugged terrain. My feet instinctively found their way, freeing my peripheral vision to attend to my surroundings.

With a gigantic leap, I hurdled the creek, and came to a flat expanse of solid rock before a vertical wall. With a sense of being nearly weightless, I scaled it with ease. Perched on the edge of the cliff, a powerful force surged up from the soles of my feet, through my body, and burst from my lungs with a mighty roar. I felt like the trees, whose roots hugged and melted over the rock. These trees maintain their tenacious hold in the most violent of storms and tap into a source of moisture and nutrition where, seemingly there is none. With this earthly connection, I felt a strong sense of belonging, and knew that no matter what is happening or where I am, I receive exactly what I need.

*a natural death is a thing of beauty.*

*In a luminescent sunset tapestry,*
*Woven with dimming light and glowing darkness,*
*A frayed silhouette of black jungle fabric*
*Is embroidered over the curtain of dusk.*

*A thin golden seam threading its way*
*down stream,*
*Hems the skirt of shadowy echoes*
*Under soft wrinkled cushions of sand*
*That have been tucked into their beds*
*for the night.*

Wind bent and storm broken.
Smoke choked and flame
charred.

Worm chewed and ant eaten.
Sun dried and drought
parched.

Still growing upward,
Always budding again,

Through the many seasons it
is uniquely carved
By the creative forces from
without and within.

*We are all*
*but cells*
*of this heavenly*
*body called earth.*

When I think I've arrived, is surely when I'm lost.

*to be oblivious*
*to the awesome mysteriousness and splendour of life is so easy.*

*Footsteps in long shadows*
*Walk a twisted weave*
*Around rocky knobs*
*In dry creek's empty sleeve.*

*Huge petrified domes*
*Oppose one another.*
*Like night and day,*
*One eclipsing the other.*

*Channelled winds guide*
*Into narrowing choices.*
*Progress announced*
*By spectating winged voices.*

*Two easy ways out*
*Are not to be taken.*
*Unknowns await.*
*Thirst for new sights awaken.*

*Empty falls and rock walls,*
*The end of the line.*
*Not turning back,*
*Impulse tackles the incline.*

*Age old worn stone*
*Echoes steep aspirations.*
*Crumbling grasps*
*Drop explosive situations.*

*With confidence shaken,*
*Trembling limbs pause.*
*Ascent continues*
*Despite these unearthed flaws.*

*Sighing in safe refuge*
*In a concave perch.*
*Out of options,*
*Climber hanging in the lurch.*

*Caught in fear's tight grasp,*
*Unable to descend.*
*A recline in the sunshine*
*Lets peace transcend.*

*In the breezy silence*
*Opened winged swallows*
*Effortlessly rise*
*From dark shady hollows.*

*Down over the edge,*
*Mind stays in the present.*
*Secure footing is reached*
*In gliding descent.*

*A new avenue*
*speaks of lofty promise.*
*One more attempt*
*At surmounting the abyss.*

*Uplifted spirits*
*Reach through fear to new heights.*
*Past obstacles*
*Give way to bold, keen sights.*

*Now on top of it,*
*New found strength in a bound.*
*In resting calm*
*Whistling whirlwind's cheers resound.*

ULURU, or more commonly, Ayers Rock, is the largest monolith in the world. It is 8.9 kilometres in circumference and its highest point is 348 metres above the surrounding desert plain. This single piece of stone, homogeneous in composition, is located near the geographic centre of Australia. I believe this site, held sacred by the Aboriginal people for at least 40,000 years, is the spiritual heart of the continent as well. The people of the Luridtja and Pitjantjatjara tribes view Uluru (the Earth Mother) as symbolic of life. Atop the Rock, in a waterhole, rests Tjukurapu, the Rainbow Serpent. Tjukurapu, the dawning of time, emerged from beneath the earth to create the different features of the landscape. By opening up to the wisdom Uluru and the nurturance mother nature has to offer us, we create the opportunity to heal our relationship with Mother Earth and stop destroying her and ourselves.

Although most of the thousands of tourists that visit Uluru each year would say there is something special about this place, not many would approach it with the reverence bestowed upon the great cathedrals or sacred temples of the world. By approaching it superficially, they deprive themselves of this vast richness. A memorable experience for many tourists is to follow a dotted white line to the highest point and sign their name in the registry. At one time, park rangers removed this book, but there was such an uproar, it had to be replaced.

The local Aboriginal people never climbed the rock. This difference reflects the disparity between Western and traditional Aboriginal cultures. Western culture, seeing itself as superior in the world, has tried to dominate and manipulate the natural environment. The Aboriginal people see themselves as having equal status with all creation, and have learned to live in harmony and cooperation with nature. To them, the land is more than something to be plundered for profit or mere physical sustenance. It serves as the written record of the Dreaming, a spiritual understanding of existence and creation.

The Aborigines' experience of metaphysical reality is not an abstract concept read about in books or talked about in church, but rather a daily experience of being at one with the earth they love and cherish like a mother. How differently would we treat the land if we experienced our spiritual wellbeing, as well as our physical sustenance, as being dependent on the quality of our relationship with it? The Aborigines' (like the Native Americans' and Kalahari Bushmen's) interdependence with the land is clearly demonstrated by the meaningless direction their lives take once they are forcibly divorced from their traditional relationship with it.

It appears to have been the intention of Western culture to tame the wilderness. Just as the spirit of the wild animal must be broken in order to tame it, so it is with the land. When the wilderness is taken out of the land, the spirit must go dormant. To crush the spirit of the land is to crush the spirits of the people who perceive themselves as being spiritually one with that land. Could it be that nearly all the people of the world have had their spirits tamed? Have most of us become domesticated into being like sheep, cows and chickens?

In this time of environmental crisis, there is a great need for us to draw on the knowledge of the indigenous peoples of the world — to help us respect Mother Earth, and listen to her needs so we can work and grow together with her in harmony and abundance. Human consciousness can be described as the sum total of all individual thought and perception, regardless of cultural origin. A healthy human race requires balance among the different aspects of our consciousness.

Up to this point in time, a vast majority of world consciousness has been dominated by a male, Western European style of thinking, a predominantly rational, analytical, literal, competitive, controlling,

scientific, aggressive and achievement-oriented type of thinking. This way of thinking sees everything as being separate, rather than being part of a whole. It is "I-thou" thinking rather than "we" thinking. The proliferation of this type of thinking has occurred at the expense of the more feminine, and indigenous types of consciousness, which are predominantly intuitive, artistic, ritualistic, symbolic, mystical, circular, receptive, cooperative and wholistic. As we allow these diverse aspects of ourselves equal status, then who knows what new possibilities may arise out of this synthesis?

We can also see this shift in the emergence of the Women's movement, in the growing interest among many westerners in Eastern religions and philosophies, adherence to Native American and Australian Aboriginal teachings, the gradual liberation of oppressed people throughout the world, and the land rights movements in New Zealand and Australia for the indigenous people. Even Science is developing a more circular, mystical view of the universe, as seen in the evolution of Biology and Environmental Science, and in the field of atomic physics.

We now know that as rainforests in South America are cut down, the whole planet is affected. We now know, through quantum physics, that the observer of subatomic particles directly affects the observed nature of those particles. In Psychology, we have realized that we are products of our social

environment and that many of our behaviours are part of circular patterns that form an ecosystem of interaction with others.

A big step was made in 1985, when the Land rights for Uluru were returned to the traditional owners. They, in turn, lease the land to the National Park Service and supervise the management of the park. The resort community of Yalara was officially completed in 1984 and provides all styles of accommodations for visitors.

I stayed in the Yalara campgrounds while visiting Uluru and Katajuta (The Olgas). On my second

day, I travelled in the dark to watch the sunrise awaken Uluru. Because of its huge mass, Uluru can create its own weather, which may differ from the surrounding desert plain. As light began to leak over the horizon, I could see a blanket of fog covering the sleeping giant. A steady wind blew from the south, and entered the aura of the Rock, forming a dense cloud. On the north side, the fog rolled off and dissipated into the clear sky.

The cold wind bit into my exposed hands, and found its way up my pant legs and shirt sleeves. I hadn't brought much clothing with me, knowing that it would quickly warm once the sun came up. Instead of trying to escape the wind, I climbed a tree and embraced its driving force. I felt like a sailor standing watch atop the mast, waiting with watchful anticipation for land to make its appearance on the horizon. The exhilaration warmed me from within. Rays of red light bolted across the land of the

Dreamtime, awaking Uluru from her grey slumber. Her face shone with rosy cheeks, while she rested beneath the fluffy blanket of fog. Not until the day had warmed sufficiently did she throw the blanket off completely.

I spent the morning wandering around the base of the Rock, sitting in various spots to meditate or relax in the sun. I snooped around, taking photographs of its sculptural form. Early in the afternoon I crawled into a small cave-like structure. A large plate of rock had cleaved off and slid down the face, forming a lean-to type structure. I sat in this narrow sanctuary and leaned against the cool rock.

Relaxing in hallowed silence, I felt a sense of awe, similar to entering the sanctified vastness of an old cathedral as a young boy. My stone backrest seemed to warm and soften, like an old overstuffed chair by a warm fireplace. The growing comfort coaxed me into a state of drowsiness. Tears moistened my eyes, as vague images of anticipated life-long loneliness and failure surfaced from hidden recesses of my mind. Some unseen power was urging me to lose conscious control. As I nodded off, these words came from my lips:

I am the Rock

I am of the Earth
I am of the Sky
I am always here
I am here for you
I am Great Grandmother

Come sit at my feet
And hear the truth
You are wonderful and loved
Come sit on my lap
And know you are always cared for
You are my children

I am the Rock
I am Great Grandmother

I sobbed with tears of joy and pain, feeling like I'd finally returned home after a long time away. The waves of emotion gradually subsided into a deep silent peace. I had no awareness of time passing, but when I emerged from my sanctuary, shadows cast by the dry grass and low shrubs stretched long over the sandy soil. I leisurely found my way to a vantage point where I could view the changing colours of Uluru dance at dusk.

That evening and through the days that followed, I felt relaxed and calm. I was satisfied by simple things, like walking or sitting in my natural surroundings. I had no desire to eat or drink out of boredom. I didn't even feel the need to run around and take photographs or keep myself busy. My interactions with people were easy and relaxed. I saw how most of my activity and consumption is an attempt to appease that empty/lonely feeling inside. The more I try to fill that emptiness by those means, the more disconnected I feel from myself and the world around me. By not holding my life, or the world I live in, as sacred, I cut myself off from experiencing the sense of wholeness (holiness) I long for.

Uluru stands as a monument to the magnificence of this planet; of which each of us is an integral part, with an integral role to fulfill. We realise our own magnificence when we fulfill that role. This is done by honouring the sacred wisdom of our open and uncluttered hearts, thereby discovering what truly brings us our deepest sense of inner peace. Learning to be at peace with ourselves is like coming home to a harmonious reunion with all of creation.

## INDEX OF PHOTOGRAPHS